Northside Cries
and
Lullabies

Northside Cries
and
Lullabies

by

N.V. Torres

GOODBYE PUBLISHING HOUSE

GOODBYE PUBLISHING HOUSE

First Edition, 2010
ISBN: 978-0-578-05067-6

Copyright © 2010 by N.V. Torres
All rights reserved. No part of this book may be reproduced or transmitted in any form or by any means without prior written permission of the author.

Exterior design by Aslin V. Designs © 2010.
All photos taken by N.V. Torres except photo on page 74 and back cover photo.

Printed in the United States of America.

Other books by N.V. Torres:

I Know All The Right Things To Say – 2007
ISBN: 978-0-6151-4883-0

For Julio, Joshua, Nasasha, Selena, Angelica,
Aliyah, Melanie, Juan, Jacob, Danny Jr., Makayla, Hailie, Isaiah,
Amelia, Chulo...

and for North Philly -
For so long you were the only one who knew.
Now everyone will know.

It's only a paper moon
Sailing over a cardboard sea,
But it wouldn't be make-believe
If you believed in me.
-- Ella Fitzgerald, *It's Only A Paper Moon*

Contents

Acknowledgments

1 a.m.	1
Haiku 1	3
North Star	4
Un Cigarrillo, la Lluvia, y Tu	5
Broken	7
Under the El	9
Time is Dead	11
Haiku 2	13
Bullets Over Hope Street	14
Downtown	16
11:12	18

The Diamond Collector	20
Tired.	21
Wino	23
For Clyde	25
Adonis	27
Damsel, Distressed	29
Like the Movies	32
The Suffering	33
?	34
Haiku 3	35
Outside My Window	36
I Am Latina	38
A Poem for My Mother	40
PT	42
This is Meant to be Spoken	44
Freezer Burn	46
In the A.M.	47
Tonight I Can Afford Freedom	49
More Better Blues	51

Nightly Ritual #101	53
You, Me, and my mangled Heart	54
Sweet Tea	56
Take Me On	59
Nightly Ritual #102	60
Any time, Any place	61
Shhh	62
Haiku 4	63
Venus	65
Glossy	66
Spaghetti (Mom's Style)	68
Artists	70
The Zoo	72
When We Were Superheroes	75
On the Stoop	77
Sick	78
Binoculars	81
The Outcome of What Comes Out	83
The Numbing Cycle	86

I-76	88
Message for the Unloved	90
9 Days of Rain	93
Haiku 5	94
Kensington Avenue	96

Acknowledgments

All of my love goes out to the following:

God – May you continue to spill your light over me;

Mom – Thank you for teaching me the kind of love that will carry me through the rest of this world;

My brothers Wes, Rick, Danny and Frank; My sister Julissa Torres; The Marcilio Children; The Ortiz Family; My beautiful family and friends – Thank you for your endless support;

Michael, Joseline, Steph, Helen, Fred, Nashira, Ebony, Jason, M.R., and Angel – Thank you for your friendship...Thank you for believing;

Christian, Michelle, P, and Kev – Thank you for contributing your talents to this collection;

And to all the gifted writers and storytellers who have helped me become better – You all deeply inspire me...Thank you.

I cannot tell the truth about anything unless I confess being a student, growing and learning something new every day. The more I learn, the clearer my view of the world becomes.

-- Sonia Sanchez

1 a.m.

Unwrap myself under
a velvet night
Moon sneaking a glimpse
through my window
shining pure light on
walls that enclose me

hombre de oro,
I lay on this bed
collected,
wistful and
mentally inhaling
visions of you

Thoughts build up to
uncover curves
bitten lips

and hips
   while my hand slips
      down
searching for your touch
yearning your presence -
pleasure for freedom...

and finally
releasing
a song that echoes all I have
ever wanted to say and do
to you.

Haiku 1

                                        I love him so much

                that I hide his boots each night

so he cannot leave

North Star

Do you know what I know?
That tonight a virgin gave birth to a mighty man.
People will gather
in churches;
homes and alleys
I will gather...
cozy and calm wishes for you.

I wish
to catch the North Star and
put it in your pocket
for guidance;
for an easier path towards you.
Your light is going dim, baby
but your rum is still so good.
And in the glow of a lit tree
      (red, yellow and green)
I hope you found
what you were searching for.
I hope
she is holding you right.

Merry fucking Christmas, baby...
Wherever you are tonight.

Un Cigarrillo, la Lluvia, y Tu

Thoughts were rapid and frigid
as I attempted to inhale the smoke, the moon
and your presence all in the same breath.

I expected the rain -
a five day forecast told me so
but I did not expect your wet
boots on my porch.
You said you walked thirteen blocks
in the rain to talk
and to bum a cigarette.
So you bummed, you talked,
and I listened.

You said something about thinking too much
and wanting to let God in –

you wanted to lead Him into the
dark room in your heart.
You laughed at the thought of
Jesus dying for our sins
and cried as you spoke of his resurrection.
You mumbled on about life, war
and contemplated the movement of clouds –
    "Where are they going?"
I just listened, dazed
while a fucked up combination of words and
smoke escaped the space between your lips.

I could not say anything
Just stood there with my back against the wall
watching the street lights flicker,
and wondering...

Somehow I am certain
that we will find ourselves in the exact same spot tomorrow
You - awaiting God
And I - anticipating a dose of clarity.
Yes, tomorrow
con un cigarrillo, la lluvia
y tu.

Broken

(Collaboration with **Christian Alvarez**)

For every broken heart never loved in return, I say to you
Time and cheek rolled tears make these words true and real
And for all the nights you stood broken
Know that many suns will rise to shed light onto the one who wants you near
In the middle of the darkest night
In the deepest of the soundest sleep
In dream
I search
for questions instead of answers
I search for a familiar face
I search for you and only you
My only
if only
you

But still
Dreams are only dreams
and the reality of my hand in your hand
is what keeps me going

You are the one that drives me home
A rainy window I peek through and stare at sun stars far away but you are so close
Almost within reach

The feel of a woman's skin is unlike any felt fingertip
And I take
advantage
I can't resist
falling into every inch of you
Lost in the thought of what you might taste like
Lost in the ways you won't turn away
The things I could do if only allowed

Will you let me touch what I have been craving for?
You make me feel so real
Never seen and
Still
arrived,
taken apart,
never, and first
With you I make sense
and I believe
I believe in you and me
as if I've been there, done that
Maybe in dreams
you are my each and every thing.

Under the El

Standing on empty streets
as a dirty breeze blows in my face
I reflect on Love's glorious matter
Tangible like everlasting petals
Yet distant
like an ice storm in July

Above me,
Lovers elevate into the sky
above buildings, above all;
> Flying in circles
> Singing with the birds
> Dancing on rainbows and
> Feasting on butterflies...

And I,
with both feet still
on the pavement,

I wait on the avenue
Counting tumbleweeds of trash
and of broken glass
Knowing that somewhere
      Dust is collecting on pillows
      Flowers go unwatered
      A delicate heart is caged
While I stand
under the El train
waiting for a hurricane

waiting for him.

Time is Dead

Yesterday's prayers wither like the hours
The hands fading out the crescendo of hope
A young girl playing dress up,
First day of school - seeds in soil
Today is new,
but it is stiff and numb

Caught in the grit of January
and sorely wanting April.

Haiku 2

On cold stormy days

        clouds clear the way to create

a new horizon

Bullets Over Hope Street

Bullets over Hope Street
Break like a rock against a window -
like goose bumps.
Bleed under a purple sky
And stroll to a busted beat.

Bullets over Hope Street
Smell like weed and bus pollution
Bitter like Olde E
Ring like hungry spoons against empty plates
Speak with a Spanish accent
Sweet like the first cries of a baby
Hard like a cold park bench
Yet as easy as a pill.

Bullets over Hope Street
Are long like welfare lines
As stale as the last slice of bread
Lurk like a stray cat
and shine like pennies on the ground.

Bullets over Hope Street
Sting like rage against minds
(the greatest minds you have ever known)

And sleep like island dreams
weighing heavily on the eyelids of viejitos.

Bullets over Hope Street
Release - fly like birds
And are the mothers -
the keepers of prayers,
dreams and wishes
for a different,
and brand new tomorrow.

Downtown

The rain came down hard that night;
crashed into the ground.

Street lights reflected on puddles underneath my heels
and we hurried upon
the downtown sidewalks -
all the glory of youthfulness oozing out of our pores.

It was 2:00 am
when we left the warm,
inviting embrace of disco lights for
dry shelter under a cold,
lonely awning;
We waited for the rain to falter.

Somewhere in between our failed attempts to hail a cab
and calming the cosmos nesting blissfully
in my stomach,
I discovered an older woman draped in heavy rags
sleeping on the concrete
next to the subway entrance.

The damp cardboard
resting on her torso read
"God Bless America"
in the thickest black letters I had ever seen.

      She was there.

      And I saw her.

      We ALL saw her.

But all we could remember
was the weight of the rain coming down that night;
crashing
into the ground.

11:12

And he will never know or understand just how beautiful he is to her...a luminous source of light to the deep vessels of her being. She walks...alone - coming from work, school, the corner bodega...always alone. She makes a wish every night at 11:11. And unlike time, she stops and she waits. She is loyal to him even in the worst weather. She is...always.

Yet,
there is pain. And silence...and more silence.
And there are poems...and more poems...and more of this: letters that make no sense, like letters to a horse.

He will never read this. And she knows that - he will never understand...
because there is still so much that needs to be said...lips that need to be pressed...turn back the clocks. Return to that basement in Fern Rock - the night she didn't want to leave but he had to work in the morning. She remembers

getting into the cab as he sat on the porch, hoodie over his head, soaking in the night.
She misses him.

And she wants.
She wants to wake up with his hands in her hair instead of his voice over the phone - some days he is just an e-mail in her inbox. She wants to drown her sorrow with his love instead of with Arizona Green Tea because after a while the pain floats back up to the surface.

And she wants to be brave and say the things that will either make or break their hearts.

She misses him.

The Diamond Collector

Some men are like diamond collectors;
they go searching -
mining for diamonds;
a precious jewel that will make them feel good.

Once they find one that they like,
they shine it up,
make it bling,
make it feel good about itself;
Then they put it in their pocket -
as oppose to wearing it on a ring or necklace.

No...
they go off searching for more stones and
they put it in their pocket,
just in case...

just
in
case.

Tired.

I want
Someone
Someone who wants me on a different level
A high and deep level

I want long conversations about life and love
Not meaningless text/email/phone messages
Phone sex

I want to hold hands
Not have hands wandering
Trespassing

I want questions
like *"Where did you grow up?"* and
"Where do you see yourself in 5 years?"
NOT
"What is your bra size? Oh and, do you swallow?"

I want flowers
not condoms and recommendations of
"really good" porn flicks

I want someone who will call me by my name and
who won't call me 'ma' or 'sweetheart'

I want...

I want someone who actually listens

Not someone who studies the movement of my lips and wonders about the great things that I can do with them

I want to be respected

and wanted

for what is inside

and not have to worry about those who

just want to come inside...literally

I want more

Need more than the physical

I need a spark

I need a fire that was not started by the heat between bodies

but by the connection and powers of two minds

Two hearts

I want to stop searching for smoke signals

and for once

let them find me

I want

No games

No sex

Just

us.

Wino

Crusty cry

Bourbon on his lip

He stumbles the streets of the night, of the days

Counting the cracks

While breaking his momma's back

How she rolls over in her grave from the sight of him now

Oh, another night of

Feeding for the beast in his belly

How its growling whine

Keeps him up at night

Holes in his pockets

Its another night of gathering

nickels from the tracks

and those whispers

(oh, those whispers)

Spilling truth in his ear:

    "What ever happened to you?!"

He looks up at the stars with watery eyes
and drifts back to times when pain was tolerable
Times when the ache in his gut didn't burn as much
Swallow a couple tabs of Rolaids
and it was gone
just like that!

From a distance
A street lamp glazes his forehead
with light
He closes his eyes
and remembers
the freckled face little girl he walked out on
So many, many moons ago.

For Clyde

(Dedicated to a true F.R. gangster)

(Allow me to write these words for when I am finished with them I will fold this poem into a paper plane and send it your way...)

He said we did not give it our all
and if we really wanted it
we would already have it.
I listened closely
pressing the phone tightly against my ear as if he was
telling me a secret.

He,
Who never hummed the melody of a sad song,
He,
Who painted the city sky yellow when I wanted it black,
He,
Whose soul smelled like sweet lilies that night I rested my
head on his lap
He is
extraordinary.

He is the hope that I see in North Philly murals
The goodness in a deed forgotten
He is the gentle kiss of a lover carrying chocolates and
flowers

And
the only one who came to my rescue the one night I wanted
to spill my life down the bathroom sink.

He saves and he doesn't have an "S" on his chest.
He feeds hope from his hand
and not the kind that went sour in the pantry
but the kind of hope that grew with love in his pocket.
He believes.
But most importantly,
He loves life and
Because he loves life
I do too.

The city lights have dimmed since you left, Clyde
Come back soon...

Adonis

Let me hold you, beautiful one
Let me place you in familiar arms like
that time many years ago
when I found you
sleeping below the tree that delivered you.

Allow me to worship your footprints on the soil
Count every strand of your hair
Forgive me,
but I love to watch you hunt
And the way you ride my chariot into the dawn
is enough to drive this goddess insane
in lust

So lets
hurry
Before this day is done
Before time slips
and makes way for another cold

season without you

Let us
escape
the oddness of the underworld
      bleed what I bleed
I am the last drop of wine on your lip
You had me at first taste

I am
your only
Don't ever forget that,
my love.

Damsel, Distressed

I never claimed that I could save you.
All I really want to do is hold you
I will save you once you save me from
this numbing sensation in the heart -
on the edge of being devoured by a true fire-breathing
dragon who calls himself Life.

> *Where is my Man behind shining armor whose*
> *sole purpose is to protect?*

Rescue me from the system of these things
From the blankets of layered cynicism,
One over another, smothering me
Head to toe.

You know,
Every blue moon,
I escape and call for Him in the gloom,
    Sweet song of deliverance
But no answer.

I throw a bone,
Sometimes two,
    lovely ones
But He does not bite.

Perhaps now it is too late and He has found refuge in the bed of another
He found his One.

After all,
Who can resist when *she* has diamonds in her eyes.
But He never claimed that He could save me...
Still, He never tries.
I just keep expecting Him to
While I cling on the
tongue of Life.

Like the Movies

blissfully unaware of conscience substances departing swiftly in the wind / her eyes, beams of sunshine / luminous in a parallel world / universally transparent to gray matter / he takes her hand into his own / all of the despair of the cold world sinking into her lips / in desperation to kiss him / the movie begins / the presence of God before them as muscles and vessels become quiet for the first time in countless moons / constant measures and pressures to revive a life from solitude and emptiness / the credits roll / his hand becomes idle / and suddenly all hope of an everlasting affair with love has left the atmosphere via the exit door.

The Suffering

The night is deep and wide -
An artery
Pulled and bleeding

Tonight is a dirty mirror
and he is a man
staring into the face of someone who
once loved a woman
swollen with love poems

She was a damsel - in wreck
And he wore armor for just one night

After the fire
He was no hero, just dessert
Merely a line in one of her poems
        Blood on her teeth

He did not put up a fight
welcomed the suffering

At daybreak,
she grew wings and left
But not empty-handed

She took a rib.

?

Am I supposed to lie down for you?
Tell me
Who are you?
A man worthy?
Show me

What makes you different?
What makes your taste sweeter than the others?

Show me the capability of your hands
because words are like paper planes
these days they sometimes fall short

Show me the capability of your hands

Are they rough
and honest?
Patient?
Can they build for something?
Rock a baby to sleep?
Tell me what makes you different?

Who the fuck made you the **one**?

Haiku 3

The streets are calling

            Red and blue lights wait for you

Don't pick up the phone

Outside My Window

Outside my window,
There are no hummingbirds
No creeks or tadpoles
A broken sunshine greets me everyday
or sometimes the occasional "YO! Vanessa!"

Outside my window,
Old men sit in the company
of a nice cold Bud
checking out the pretty young thang
strutting by
in her skin tight jeans
and flashy gold hoops with her name in the middle
You know,
just in case he forgets.

Outside my window,
Children play Tag on cracked sidewalks
A melody rolls up the street
and they run like roaches into their homes
to get a dollar from their momz for ice cream
Sometimes a $1.25 if you want jimmies

Outside my window,
I hear a car radio system that rattles

my screen door every god-damn time!
I wonder:
"How can all that come from this tiny Honda?!"
> *Some pendejo wants to get noticed...*

Outside my window,
The women of the block
sit out on their stoops
and gossip about the lady next door who
was fighting with her husband last night
at 3:30 a.m.
Even though their eyes were closed,
their ears were wide open

Outside my window,
a crackhead
tries to sell me a gold link chain for twenty dollars
I can tell by his eyes
he wants to use the money to go around the corner
and buy his poison
Feed his addiction

Outside my window...

> *Don't feel sorry for me,*
> *This is who I am...*

> *Don't feel sorry for me,*
> *This is who I am.*

I Am Latina

(Collaboration with **This_isjust_M**)

Do you see me and know who I am?
Can you hear and sense where I've been?
Will you judge my cover before you take a look in?
I am Latina and I am here

I will raise my daughter to be independent and strong
Teach my son the difference between right and wrong
Educate myself and allow in knowledge to make me better
Inspiration from this generation who refuse to be held back
Here we come with a vengeance feel this Taino attack

I know what you think when you see my walk
Your whispers about my body, my lips and the way I talk
The empowerment of my sisters is what you fear
Because I am Latina and I am here

Do you see me and know who I am?
Would you listen to what I say?
Can you handle the power of my sway?
I am Latina and I am here

I was born to love with my whole heart
Learned to overlook degrading remarks
Developed a strong mind and soul from the very start

I live to make my ancestors proud
Sing the melody of my island out loud
I celebrate my beauty every minute, day, and year
Because I am Latina and I am here

Now when you see me don't be quick to assume
We are a culture of pride which started from the womb
I've been taught strength and have the power to persevere
I am Latina and I am here

And from the top of a mountain I shout out
To las mujeres who know what being Latina is all about
Watch our hair blow loosely with the breeze
As our curvy bodies make men weak in the knees
Our potential to have it all is what you fear
So take notice and unclog your ears

We are Latinas and we are here.

A Poem for My Mother

I am writing this to you
with hands that promise to be useful
Not solely for writing poems,
wiping tears
and making love
Because they are just hands
that will one day learn to
warm milk for little ones
Clean grains of rice
and build roots
outside
where my wishes grow
fast like weeds after April showers

I dream of a place - a home
where I will lay my heart and feet
live, create
and breathe until there is nothing left
I have dreams where these hands are not yours
but mine

entirely

and free

free...

I am writing this poem because

these dreams of a different home

will dismantle walls and tear down cities

Dance along the edges -

loosely and gradually

but these hands will never forget

the warmth - Always remember

the sacrifice

body, tears, and blood

I

will never forget that

you

were

my first home.

PT

I hate waiting for the bus.
Especially on busy streets.

Stand there waiting, mad as fuck while a bunch of assholes drive by staring at you. As if they have never seen someone waiting for the bus.

Sometimes I get so enraged that I wish I had a middle finger tattooed on my forehead so I can secretly say **"Fuck off! Stop staring asshole!"** without actually saying it because, you know, that would be really rude.

This is Meant to be Spoken

And this is meant to be spoken.
I heard a song today that asked why love sometimes feels like a battlefield. A battered land of warriors, holding their lover's heart in their bare hands. Savages. But you - you are a poet. Whether you feel it or not, your heart shelters a beast - sleepy and collective now, but fierce and resilient when awaken. Like I always say: When in Love or in Lust, we are simply animals. Nearly civilized. The body always wants what it cannot hold. And I don't know if you understand what I'm saying. This is meant to be spoken. This is meant to meet you halfway. To hold you. Calm the belly of the beast and tell you that I'm still here. Living. Ready and scared, but eager. Not like a warrior. Like a poet. My offering is rich and only comes in one flavor. My breast and hips are ripe. Warm sweet milk for tiny mouths. But I am getting ahead of myself now. Do you understand? This is meant to be spoken. Yesterday, I confessed my secrets to an old man in a cardboard box as he chanted aloud "A CHANGE IS COMIN' ON....OH CHANGE, COME ON"! And you probably won't believe me when I say this, but I believe him. These leaves will rust come September. And though I like to think that it is deeper than autumn leaves, you've

failed to paint me a different picture. I want to see you, one morning, as you embrace the new sky and expand the edges, spreading them wide and thin. And at that very moment I will pray that no one ever takes it away - your live and smiling spirit. Understand? I don't want to wake up early another morning yearning for the warm sighs of possibilities on my neck. I like to sit on the edge - simmering in the palm of Love waiting to be swallowed. I apologize if I lost you. I just want you to know that you don't have me fooled. Under your skin, tucked away is the truth. Rotting words that have lived for ages - passed down to you from generations before your time like an unwanted piece of furniture. A burden. And those words have learned to settle, comfortably, in the center of who you are - just waiting. Waiting for a lady, a poet like me, to come and stir them into a boiling soup. Sip slow, love. We are beautiful.

This is beautiful.

Freezer Burn

I came across myself today...

There I was
Reflecting in a cup of coffee
Familiar lines,
eyes
staring back, pupils
engaged-
Turbulent thoughts playing tag
in my head again:
      silly rabbit
      don't you know love
      is for fools
(I want to be a fool, too)
      I want to be a fool too...
Warm porcelain on
dry palms,
I walk to the
kitchen
open the freezer

This coffee needs to
cool down a bit.

In the A.M.

In the a.m.
I am here
feeling lonely
needy
ready to give up on everyone
and everything in my life.

In the a.m.
I am here
and at this exact time
three little boys die in a fire

Sleep sweetly angels.

Tonight I Can Afford Freedom

(Collaboration with **Christian Alvarez** - written on the night of November 4, 2008)

In the days to come
Things will be questioned but today is the day of change
An evening of chance and impression for the world.
In the days to come
Opportunity will speak
Bells will ring
and the people will reinvest their hearts into
a land that forgot

In these days to come smiles will return
Expectations will gain weight
And the evils of the world will feel the chilling winds of
change on weathered faces

In these days to come children will look down
at their hands and see not color
but water - reflections of the future
and esperanza
Because right now there is nothing in the world but this
moment

A hope filled now
Not seen unless afforded in way too long
Freedom has gathered in Chicago
and the world waits for its chosen chance
They wait for flowing tears
And spoken words that will light up the sky
Words that will make
h i s t o r y.

More Better Blues

Baby,
you give me more better blues
The kind that sits around and lingers
in the bedroom where we used to.....

Its the kind that keeps my eyes wet, sore;
my heart withered and cold;
my wineglass full.
It's the kind that answers your phone
asking "Hello?"

I say,
baby its blue because it isn't red!
It isn't us
Our fire
you and I.
Take these blues away
I'll trade them in for a lighter shade
a sunny white day

where you know the right things to say.
If you were here,
I'd put your hands and mouth to good use
Your hands will wipe these tears away
and your mouth will utter two little words.

But,
you give me more better blues
Keeps my pen busy for weeks
    nights
trying to decipher all of this blue you've placed upon me
    haunting me
Sitting in a smoky room
congested with all that you had to say
and all that I did not want to hear.

Nightly Ritual #101

Reading Bukowski before bed.

I lay back, put the TV volume really low, open the book and start reading from where I left off the night before.

Ten minutes later, I am passed out – too lazy and sleepy to turn off the light.

I don't know what it is, but my eyes always get heavy every time I read him.

And I actually enjoy reading his work.

You, Me, and my mangled Heart

There is nothing as tragic as being swept up then let down by love.
And for you, sir I was carried away...

You see,
For love, I hitched a rocket to the moon and
peeled my rugged skin on the surface
I awaited the sunlight -
Allowed the rays to soak my mangled heart so I could love you
I recharged and drifted back to earth,
Settled my gun and feet on the ground and
into the soil to inhale the sweet lilies once again
For I missed the colors of true love in the sky
Though a thousand miles high - Unreachable and wild
I opened up and
left it all behind for a speck of glitter in your eye
and for your right hand on my thigh
I fed you my love with a silver spoon
I sang stories about the moon to you.

However,
you wanted to go straight to dessert -
You wanted to taste and kiss the stars
so I watched as you licked and savored every drop
And come morning,
like a true loner,
you traveled on.

But still,
For love, I carry on
I seek and roam
Spread, speak,
think and know
You are the closer,
the opener,
and the mangler of this awful yet beautiful sensation
And unfortunately for me,
I will never forget you.

Sweet Tea

My lover from the northside

has gone to pick me flowers from my neighbor's garden

My honey boy, sticky and fresh

tangerine lips

How can I forget?

A smile that I feel somewhere deep

tickles my feet

Lost in his eyes

open spaces

where my heart is free to fly,

my lover from the northside...

made me breakfast while I was still in bed

Eggs, toast with jelly

and a nice hot cup of tea

'Extra sugar, please!'

Sipped his love slowly

Like the hymns of the pigeons outside

Momma said he seems like a good guy

And his hands never do lie,

my lover from the northside...

isn't as tough as he appears

Not stone-cold, grim

Yes, the boy loves his Timbs
but when the boots come off -
under my bed
He is the perfect shade of red
Passionate and gentle at the same time
I'm a mosquito
and his sweet blood makes my tongue cry,

my lover from the northside -

his love spreads far
from here to Crooklyn
Feels like warm milk spilling in
He carries this poem in his back pocket
Understands the similes and metaphors -
says 'baby, I got it'
And on Sundays we lay
while the city's melody plays
Are those fireworks I hear
or bombs coming down?
It doesn't matter
Its calm in here

for now.

Take Me On

(It came and then it went...but still I meant every word)

Love came quietly

like Sunday -

a slow burning bed.

Love came between -

sinking into bones

steady and

ready,

mad and

still

Love came...

Nightly Ritual #102

Undressing for bed in my room and striping down to just panties.

I soon realize that I have to pee...badly.
...sigh, of course.

Covering my bare breast, I make the walk to the bathroom, do my thing and head back to my room and into my bed.

I know one night I will get caught going to the bathroom half naked.

The weird part is that I don't really care if I do.

Any time, Any place

I can take you
    in the copy room

You may have me
    on the teacher's lounge couch
    or in the janitor's closet

Slippery when wet...

    Caution: I will let you have me any time...any place.

Shhh

Secret:

I have 4 freckles
on my inner
right thigh -

Wanna connect the dots?

Haiku 4

I hear birds chirping

from the comfort of your bed -

Time for me to go

Venus

Mouth against heart,
against hips
We are parallel - one
as your lips absorb the taste of my fever

Eager hands journey south
to the knees
north,
up the thighs
            i n s i d e

I am Venus
and you, mister...

      You are divinity.

Glossy

Saturday nights spread thickly
like lip gloss
A sheer, pink shade that shimmers
beneath the lights
sending a violent heat wave
across the bar
when
trouble walked in with
boots
knee-high
and full lashes

all
eyes
on...

her.

She
made us stop
and take notice
She
made me wish...

wish my breast could know the sun

the same way this girl
knows danger -
the way she plays with fire
Igniting flames in the snugged parts of each man she passes
Inhaling the howls
and sipping on the heavy pants
sloppy
wet

glossy

I watch the
spectacle from afar
soaking in my own
mire of insecurities and
wondering

How much that kind of freedom would cost...

On any given rainy day,
how many pennies would I have to save
to buy that kind of power
with legs closed?

Spaghetti (Mom's Style)

Just a thought...

One day, I want to come home from work and feed my children. Cook dinner - my favorite: spaghetti...Mom's style. I want to help the kids with their homework, feed the dog...and cat. Sit in the dining room and balance the checkbook. Pay some bills online. Call my mom while the kids clean their room. Afterwards, we'll take a walk around the neighborhood with the dog. Come home just in time for Wheel of Fortune. Get the kids ready for bed when it's over. Two baths and one bedtime story later, I walk into the living room and find my husband sitting on the couch catching the last few minutes of the Sixer's game.

I want to sit next to him - place one hand on his lap. Turn off the TV in disappointment. Kiss his bottom lip, and ask, "*Are you hungry?*" He would ask, "*What's for dinner?*", and I would reply "*Spaghetti...Mom's style.*" At that moment his eyes would light up, and with a slight half smile, he would say:

"I'm starving."

Artists

(For my partner in art - because this is who we are and who we'll always be)

I am slipping
into a black hole in the universe
where insecurities and solitude call my name.
They want me to retreat,
sit, and share a cup of coffee and cigarette.
To my surprise (well, not really)
You were invited also.
You see,
You and me,
We have this thing where,
as artists,
We feel what most people can not touch
We think about shit that people want to leave alone
And we dream in a place where the sun attempts to peak her head.
We connect, my friend
my comrade.

We can retreat here together, you know.
This could be it!
It could start with you reaching inside of me
and cradling my pain in your bare hands
Speak to it;
Sing it a song in words that only we know;

Nothing silly, please!
Because I am serious...
We can make this our home.

We will fill our bellies with Puerto Rican rum,
Sleep on water stained cots;
Waste away our nights and days
staring at the walls,
talking, talking,
thinking, painting...
Cook up a mixture of our blood and oil colors
and use them to paint a picture of a city we both love and hate!
And who knows...
Maybe one night, out of pure drunkenness,
you will leave pieces of yourself in my womb
making me the bearer of a new generation willing to carry
on the ways of our life

My friend
We are spilling!
Slowly spilling into a black hole in the universe
Where our solitudes call for us;
But I have to say
it feels really good
to have you by my side.

The Zoo

(Collaboration with **Irwin Roman**)

It's about that time again
I'm thinking again
I keep trippin'
'Bout to start drinkin' again.
My feelings and memories are starting to get the best of me
Trying to make it day in day out
Wondering what's my destiny
Reminisce about the past and then I ask myself if this is how it was meant to be,
And if so, why is this the life that was given to me?

I remember when this life was good to me
When my map was direct
Easy and carefree
This road was once as smooth as the space where the ocean meets the sand,
but today I'm singing the blues to this cold glass in my hand
As the past gathers itself to find a comfortable seat in my head,
I struggle to stay afloat in the tears that I shed

Drowning in sorrows
Wishing for better tomorrows
But all I can see is visions of North Philly in my head

Gun shots, police sirens disturbing my sleep while in bed.
It's known as the Badlands;
Politicians never show face, never shake hands
Then they wonder why the hood shows no respect
Well we're treated like shit,
What more would you expect?

We come from a long history of neglect
The streets tell us to serve and protect...ourselves
from those whom we elect,
They sleep tight and peacefully
while we fight to see through the smoke and debris
From the flying bullets and bombs over row homes
Working for pennies to quiet the stomach groans

While making 6 figure salaries
Telling us what change we need
An American Dream fueled by nothing but greed
While keeping up with the Jones'
Working our fingers to the bones is all we do
But this just isn't my life, it's my hood's life too
And though at times it's not much more than a zoo,
We all try to stay strong,
survive and make it through.

When We Were Superheroes

(For Frank)

When we were heroes
We would run the landmines of the badlands
untouched
playing tag
cops and robbers, Power Rangers
(I was always the pink one)

When we were heroes
we were super
invincible figures
standing tall
marching to lullabies
Learning to fly

But now those badlands are no longer a backdrop to our
imagination,
but a reality
a cold pill
swallowed
Barricading the cries

We are walking on battled lands, my brother
with real guns and rose-colored concrete
The same color as the ones that bloomed on
the only rose bush in our neighborhood

The same color as the rose I placed
onto our uncle's casket back in '98

> *Do you remember?*
> *He was someone's hero...*

And we dodged plastic bullets in the fields that he ran
Now we dodge the temptations,
the fast cash
and wet whispers
in the same fields where mothers lose their babies
Oasis for a junkie and his pipe -
holding tight to that kryptonite

When we were heroes
We were superheroes
Innocent and
brave
Do you remember
when we could fly?

We can still fly.

On the Stoop

(Inspired by Mr. Hughes)

One does not have to pray to the sky
for answers -
How? And why?

Just sit on the stoop and listen to
the concrete echo the meaning of life:
      STAY ALIVE!
Do what you must do to survive
hustle
bustle
keep shifting those muscles
because the minute you stop
the heat drops
and the landlord knocks.

Sit on the stoop
and watch a spirit droop
to the sound of a sad drum
because sometimes to eat
one must remain a hostage of the streets -
Drown a hard day of work with a shot of liquor
and store their dreams in a pipe
to defer.

Sick

(Collaboration with **Kevon Crute**)

Writing murder with a stamp of approval...
Lullabying those who speak of manure

A microwave containing tin foil resemble my thoughts
Mirroring my mind, sending more shots
At the victims of my last sick poem, they were simple afterthoughts
Coughing out words worth the devil's discussion
Even in death there can be repercussions
Gun to my head hoping to suffer from concussion
No dice...
Popping pills of excellence for this aching of my head
"If I killed all who sin, we'd all be dead"
Boxing the face of society's face till its bloody red

Inconsistency's bullets load this chamber...
Preparing to kill these decimals looking for the remainder
And what remains of you?

Let's subtract you from the equation...
This is the kiss of death, prepare of osculation
Death waits...
Setting you a flame, seeing the fiery gates...

"This pen's more deadly...Then a bullet from Mark Chapman
Stepping on you Beatles...this had to happen"

Forgive me father for I have sinned...
I'm on a subway train to hell,
with a screaming pen
and a pretty pink grin
Who dares to stop the conductor?
Not you,
Or you...
I carry poems like blades,
Cutting right through

Even in death my words instigate wars in my mind
Gun to my head,
A trigger away from
spilling lyrical liquids onto the blind
Forcing you to observe greatness
and society's removal
Damn,
Its official
I'm writing murder with a stamp of approval.

Binoculars

Yesterday
You sent me a pair of
binoculars in a rugged box
addressed to "Poeta"
>they were shiny
>clear lenses

Attached to it
was a note explaining its purpose
and why it would benefit me
And it became clear to me:
For sure you will always remember me as the
poet who saw the world through gray
foggy binoculars...

I try
to remember the good old blue sky
And once in awhile
I manage to paint wishful visions of a collision
of good things heading my way
I try
to mentally recite the virtue of your words
and I sometimes use them
to pin my heavy curls away from my eyes
>like you always said
>*"Keep a clear vision..."*

And I try to make an effort
everyday
To structure my written words
in ways that make sense to
your eyes and ears

But not today...
Today I choose to bask in the rays of my own
ruthless shame
I choose to lounge
and write
in this obscure penthouse I like to call my head
    LET ME HAVE MY MOMENT!
To hold this pen in my hand
and revisit the scars,
Trace the dry blood with my finger tip
Like Braille on my wrists
Etched here is the story of what it used to feel like
for this poet
The story of painfully stained razors
and blurred binoculars...

So tomorrow
I will grant you a lucid vision
And my pen will return to the position you love so dearly
But today...
Today belongs to the shadows,
to my story,
and to the tint of my past.

The Outcome of What Comes Out

What comes out
>my blood
>my fruit

I have planted you

or shall I say *we*

He and I

But it is *I* who would have grown you
>nurtured you
>sheltered you

Heal your scrapes

bruises, tummy aches,

broken heart and all

Feed you milk and chocolate-chip cookies

Still,

It is I who will detach myself from you

Disconnect you from your roots
However, love you
And find strength in all that you would have become
      my seed
        a new beginning
Yet, an end.

What comes out
is a significant journey
and simple thoughts of him and I with you at the
park one clear day
watching you play.
First steps;
words;
smiles and giggles big enough to fill our days
months and years.

My child,
(because that is who you are and always will be)
What comes out
is the feeling of you
enclosed
      emptiness
And now I am regretful that I will never meet you,
hold you,
rock you to sleep,
or tell you why I will do this -
Why you can no longer grow inside of me
and enter this world

What comes out
is an ache
for the unknown
But still,
an ache
of what I have to do.

Only you know me
      my insides
         the rhythm of my heart
and the reason why, little one
this premature journey has to end here.

The Numbing Cycle

You ask,
>"*How do you feel about me?*"

I stand here wordless and
wanting to give you a response,
but I can't.
This numbing cycle -
this silent storm that is at fault
is clouding my thoughts
as words so desperately try to dodge the
dry tumbleweeds in the brain,
frantically attempting to exit the mouth
Caging the words you inevitably want to hear.

But hopefully you will discover this about me sooner
rather than later -
Rather than two seconds from now when you are
unwrapping someone else -
Sooner than three moons from tonight when I cannot
retrieve you.

But I do wish to say something today,
something to keep you holding on to the cliff of my being,
>   an incentive that will keep you on your sweet toes,
>   something to feed your hunger...

Yet my heart is numb,
my eyes are so weary,
and my pot is simply empty.

I close my eyes as you digest my stillness
Wash it down with a bottle of your favorite cheap whiskey
You turn to me;
Tell me my silence burns more than the juice that trickles down your throat...

> *"You burn! Your silence will gut me from the inside out until I become numb just like you...*
>
> > *just*
> >
> > *like*
> >
> > *you."*

And this is where it begins and ends...
The two of us...
Me,
untouched by the coldness of your words
And you,
slowly drowning the last tingle in your heart.

I-76

It's a long ride back to Philly
and we have not said a single word to each other.
You drive on
while I sit in the passenger seat
staring out the window trying
to avoid the sight of your face.
I can feel you looking over at me.
It's a long ride back.

The highway is empty at 4 in the morning
My mind and eyes are heavy
And you -
You continue to drive.

I look over to your window.
From a distance
I can see the Roxborough Towers.
I remember us
driving down this same road one night and asking you,
"Baby, what are those?"
as I pointed to the sea of blinking red lights.
You told me that they were signal towers for TV and radio.
And I remember how I attempted to
etch into my memory
the beautiful side view of you

driving into the night with those
lights shining like stars in the background.

Now here we are again
driving by.

For a moment I suspect that this
will be the last time I ever see this sight again -
You
and those fucking towers.

Our eyes meet
and I know I am right.

This will be the last time.

Message for the Unloved

The ghost
hangs outside my door,
puts out his cigarette and knocks
I can imagine the shape that his lips make as the last string
of smoke
spills into the air

The birds tell me
he is waiting now
Sweet and eager
he wants to give me a rug burn
Nice...
but no thank you

I'm not going down for anyone

But instead

with this

I will gather

words

a message for the unloved...

> *Run back towards the river*
> *Kick back and sail in your sea of missed*
> *opportunities*
> *Search for your heart*
> *Make love to your couldas*
> *shouldas, and wouldas*
> *Because I am so far gone*
> *and too slippery to hold now.*

9 Days of Rain

It was suppose to be a red

and dry season

but it rained for nine days straight this month.

Her cries were

tears over the ocean -

They did not matter to him.

And she still believes them when

they say they can make her forget.

The two things she fears more than God are

empty bedrooms

and the slow movement of a single breath.

Why stop here

when there is so much love in the world?

She can never let go

With a sweaty grip

She still holds

The last time she tried to say goodbye

She promised herself

that the next one would love her better

and wetter...

better and w e t t e r.

Haiku 5

I am colorful
She is so ordinary
Please love me instead

Kensington Avenue

For her
it is more than a road
it is an entry
An arched doorway into things unknown to her since
girlhood -
money
a warm apartment,
the love of a father or man.

For her it is a stuffer
It pays the rent
But it fills the empty spaces between the ridges
It was water under the bridges
that filled her womb
"The bump" -
that's what she calls it
It grows
and grows evenly with each slouching day and
each busy night.

For her
it was always this...
the avenue
whistles and trickles
the drip drops of random men

Piecing together the ends
because at the closing of each month
it all starts to make sense
Everyone gets what they want

But at the very end
It is always more than what money can buy
More than the dirty deeds of her pretty little mouth
It is more than
the 'cha' and the 'ching'.
She aches and needs.

She
wants
to feel open
and exposed
splattered
in the backseats
Used
but wanted.

About the Author

N.V. Torres is a Puerto Rican poet and artist from Philadelphia, Pennsylvania. Born and raised in North Philly, she has been writing poetry since the age of eleven with her very first poem being a love poem for her best friend.

Northside Cries and Lullabies is her second collection of poetry and prose. In 2007, she self-published her first collection of poems entitled *I Know All The Right Things To Say*.

Ms. Torres currently lives and in Philadelphia.

For more about N.V. Torres please visit:

www.NVTorres.webs.com

www.ItsAlwaysSunnyinNorthside.blogspot.com

www.ingramcontent.com/pod-product-compliance
Lightning Source LLC
Chambersburg PA
CBHW032049090426
42744CB00004B/143